CUSES, EXCUSES, EXCUSES, EX
CUSES   EXCUSES   EXCUSES   E

, EXCUSES,   E   SE
  EXCUSES   E   E.

CUSES, EXCUSES, EXCUSES, EX
CUSES   EXCUSES   EXCUSES   E

, EXCUSES, EXCUSES, EXCUSE
  EXCUSES   EXCUSES   EXCUSE.

CUSES, EXCUSES, EXCUSES, EX
CUSES   EXCUSES   EXCUSES   E

, EXCUSES, EXCUSES, EXCUSE
  EXCUSES   EXCUSES   EXCUSE

CUSES, EXCUSES, EXCUSES, EX
CUSES   EXCUSES   EXCUSES   E.

, EXCUSES, EXCUSES, EXCUSE
  EXCUSES   EXCUSES   EXCUSE

EXCUSES, EXCUSES, EXCUSES,
EXCUSES   EXCUSES   EXCUSES

SES, EXCUSES, EXCUSES, EXCU
SES   EXCUSES   EXCUSES   EXCU

EXCUSES, EXCUSES, EXCUSES,
EXCUSES   EXCUSES   EXCUSES

SES, EXCUSES, EXCUSES, EXCU
SES   EXCUSES   EXCUSES   EXCU

EXCUSES, EXCUSES, EXCUSES,
EXCUSES   EXCUSES   EXCUSES

SES, EXCUSES, EXCUSES, EXCU
SES   EXCUSES   EXCUSES   EXCU

EXCUSES, EXCUSES, EXCUSES,
EXCUSES   EXCUSES   EXCUSES

SES, EXCUSES, EXCUSES, EXCU
SES   EXCUSES   EXCUSES   EXCU

EXCUSES, EXCUSES

i am unable to come in to the office today because...

LISA SWERLING AND RALPH LAZAR

summersdale

EXCUSES, EXCUSES

Summersdale Publishers Ltd
46 West Street
Chichester
West Sussex
PO19 1RP
UK

www.summersdale.com

Printed and bound in China

ISBN: 978-1-84953-369-0

Substantial discounts on bulk quantities of Summersdale books are available to corporations, professional associations and other organisations. For details contact Nicky Douglas by telephone: +44 (0) 1243 756902, fax: +44 (0) 1243 786300 or email: nicky@summersdale.com.

to...

from...

Dear Mell

you have already
had a great start at
this game ...

(A) Im studying to be a
doctor

(B) Im studying to become
a doctor doctor

(C) Im having a baby

(D) I just had a baby

(E) oops. Im having a
second baby.

.... :)

So heres a few more
to add

Enjoy *Adoline*
x x

... and taken illegally
out of the country.

... and some uploads to download.

it's not that
i'm lazy

... on my website,
on facebook ...

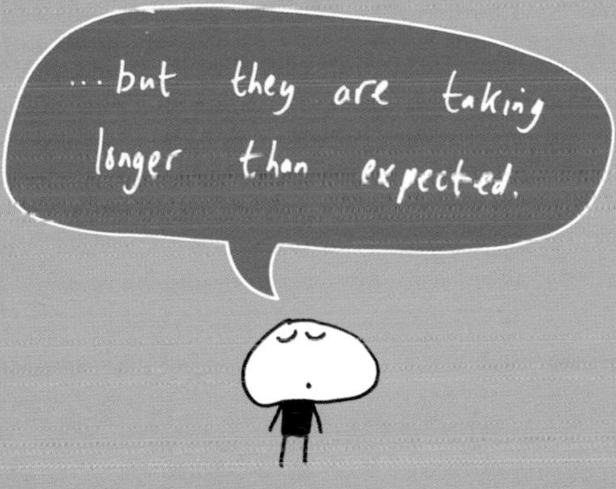
...but they are taking longer than expected.

www.mahoneyjoe.com

www.summersdale.com

EXCUSES, EXCUSES, EXCUSES, EX
CUSES   EXCUSES   EXCUSES   EX

, EXCUSES, EXCUSES, EXCUSE
    EXCUSES   EXCUSES   EXCUSE

CUSES, EXCUSES, EXCUSES, EX
CUSES   EXCUSES   EXCUSES   EX

, EXCUSES, EXCUSES, EXCUSE
    EXCUSES   EXCUSES   EXCUSE

CUSES, EXCUSES, EXCUSES, EX
CUSES   EXCUSES   EXCUSES   EX

, EXCUSES, EXCUSES, EXCUSE
    EXCUSES   EXCUSES   EXCUSE

CUSES, EXCUSES, EXCUSES, EX
CUSES   EXCUSES   EXCUSES   EX

, EXCUSES, EXCUSES, EXCUSE
    EXCUSES   EXCUSES   EXCUSE

EXCUSES, EXCUSES, EXCUSES,
EXCUSES EXCUSES EXCUSES

SES, EXCUSES, EXCUSES, EXCU
ES EXCUSES EXCUSES EXCU

EXCUSES, EXCUSES, EXCUSES,
EXCUSES EXCUSES EXCUSES

SES, EXCUSES, EXCUSES, EXCU
ES EXCUSES EXCUSES EXCU

EXCUSES, EXCUSES, EXCUSES,
EXCUSES EXCUSES EXCUSES

SES, EXCUSES, EXCUSES, EXCU
ES EXCUSES EXCUSES EXCU

EXCUSES, EXCUSES, EXCUSES,
EXCUSES EXCUSES EXCUSES

SES, EXCUSES, EXCUSES, EXCU
ES EXCUSES EXCUSES EXCU